D0875617

LOVE BEYOND DEGREE

LOVE BEYOND DEGREE

reflections to ready your heart for Easter

STARLA SHATTLER

Publishing services by Selah Publishing Group, LLC, Tennessee. The views expressed or implied in this work do not necessarily reflect those of Selah Publishing Group.

ISBN: 978-1-58930-254-9
Library of Congress Control Number: 2010905892

To the One in heaven and the ones on earth
who love me more than I could ever deserve

ACKNOWLEDGEMENTS

Books are rarely private projects, and the publishing of this manuscript has certainly been a collective effort. Many dear friends shared encouragement and excitement throughout the process, and for each of you I am thankful.

The support and generosity of my wonderful family are treasures I gratefully cherish. Words fail to express my appreciation and love, so a free copy of the book will have to do!

Neither this book nor I would be complete without my extraordinary husband. Steve, you have unselfishly loved me into being an author. Thank you—for so much. I deeply love you.

My precious daughters, Rachel, Camille, and Robin, inspire and delight me with their beaming smiles and tender hearts. I love each of you lots and lots. (You can finally tell your friends your mom finished her book!)

More than all else, this book is a work of grace. God continually stuns me with His sovereignty and His goodness. His love amazes me more each moment. These words are from Him and for Him—my gift of gratitude for His magnificent grace.

"To him who is able to keep you from falling and to present you before his glorious presence without fault and with great joy – to the only God our Savior be glory, majesty, power and authority, through Jesus Christ our Lord, before all ages, now and forevermore!" Jude 1:24-25

CONTENTS

HOW JESUS LOVED

AT THE CROSS

Alas! and did my Savior bleed,
And did my Sovereign die?
Would he devote that sacred head
For sinners such as I?

Was it for crimes that I have done,
He groaned upon the tree?
Amazing pity! Grace unknown!
And LOVE BEYOND DEGREE!

WHY JESUS CAME

LOVE
BEYOND
DEGREE

reflection 1

THE FIRST GLIMPSE

"The LORD God made garments of skin for
Adam and his wife and clothed them."

Genesis 3:21

Related Scripture
Genesis 3:1-21

They stood forlorn—trembling in fear and failure. Fig leaves are a poor camouflage for sin. The serpent had taunted and tantalized, *"Did God really say, 'You must not eat from any tree in the garden'?...You will not surely die....When you eat...you will be like God."* Eve had glanced at the fruit again. It looked good. It would taste great. It might make her a genius. How could she refuse? She couldn't. And Adam didn't.

They tried to cover up what they had done and cover over who they were. Neither worked. No amount of good could make up for the bad, for in that moment everything had changed—for the worse. Would it ever be right again? Could it ever be right again?

No more perfect garden. Adam would now fight the ground as he labored for food. Eve would now groan with pain as she labored for life. And God would not come to walk and talk in the cool of the day.

Yet even in their guilt, they were draped with grace as God protected and provided. Their fig leaf garments would rip and tear. Something better was needed, so *"the LORD God made garments of skin for Adam and his wife and clothed them."*

The lamb gasped and breathed his last.
And God took care of His children.

———————————

2 *reflection 2*

THE PREVIEW

"The blood will be a sign for you on the houses where you are; and when I see the blood, I will pass over you."

Exodus 12:13

Related Scripture
Exodus 12:1-13

"**D**addy, why are you in a hurry? Why do you have that hyssop? What will you do with the lamb? Why are we stopping at the door?" The boy's mouth moved faster than his feet as he struggled to keep pace with his father's brisk steps, so the man paused and knelt beside his son.

"Because of you, my dear one. Because of you." He pulled the lad close and continued, "Tonight the Lord will pass through Egypt and strike down the firstborn son in every family. But He has provided a way for us— for you—to be saved. If He sees the blood of a lamb, a perfect lamb, covering the doorway, He will pass over our house, and no one in it will die."

The young boy quivered and tightly grasped his father's hand.
"Have no fear, my son. Only faith. We will be saved by the blood."

The lamb gasped and breathed his last.
And God took care of His children.

———————————

3 *reflection 3*

THE MAIN EVENT

"Jesus called out with a loud voice, 'Father, into your hands I commit my spirit.' When he had said this, he breathed his last."

Luke 23:46

Related Scripture
Mark 15:22-39

With a heavy thud, the cross settled into the crude hole. Jesus lurched in pain and gasped for air. The joyous praise of adoring angels seemed eons away as His unending glory was now cruelly replaced with undeserved agony. Through the anguish, He could hear the jeers of the pious priests. *"He saved others," they said, "but he can't save himself!"*

They were wrong. And right. Oh, He could save Himself. Never wonder about that. Had He only desired, thousands of angels would have swooped to His rescue. It could have been an "off the cross and in your face" moment that silenced His accusers and delighted His followers. But Jesus couldn't save Himself and us, too.

So He chose us. *"Not my will, but yours be done,"* Jesus had prayed the night before in the garden. The Father's will was that we be saved—saved from a forever without Him. We deserve hell; He chooses to give us heaven. We deserve to be kept away; He desires for us to come near. We are guilty; He is grace.

But somebody had to pay. Almighty God cannot give and forgive without justice, or He would not be God.

He had known about it. He had planned it. He would do it. *"He himself will redeem [his people] from all their sins"(Psalm 130:8)*.

Darkness covered the earth as the price was paid.

The Lamb gasped and breathed His last.
And God took care of His children.

———————————

WHAT JESUS DID

LOVE
BEYOND
DEGREE

4 reflection 4

ON THE WAY

"Today this scripture is fulfilled in your hearing."

Luke 4:21

Related Scripture
Luke 4:1-30

Bethlehem's miracle baby grew into Nazareth's busy carpenter, and for thirty years life seemed normal. Then one day Jesus closed up shop, stepped from the shadows, and turned toward the cross.

Satan saw and tried to stop Him. Just one sin and He wouldn't be a perfect sacrifice. One small slip-up and He couldn't be a spotless lamb. A forty-day fast left Jesus weak and wanting. "Find Your strength in food. Change this stone to bread," Satan tempted. "Rule the world without redemption. Worship me, and I'll make it reality!" Satan tantalized. "Jump from this high tower. Prove You're someone big, unless You're really someone small," Satan taunted. Jesus resisted the devil's enticements with God's enduring Word and went on His way.

On Saturday, He attended church, just like always. Every Sabbath service, the priest chose five ordinary guys to read Scripture. That day he chose Jesus. Jesus stood up and read what Isaiah had written down: "God's Spirit is on me because He has sent me to cheer the poor, heal the blind, free the bound, help the hurting, and let you know that God is up to something big.'"

Jesus rolled up the scroll, gave it back to the attendant, and sat down. No one moved. Everyone watched, everyone waited, and Jesus spoke. "What you just heard is happening right now."

Their ears were open, but their hearts were closed. They recognized Him but didn't know Him. They treated Him like an ordinary Joe—the son of Joe, actually—and tried to end it all right there with a small shove off a big cliff. *"But he walked right through the crowd and went on his way."*

Temptation didn't destroy Him. Disbelief didn't distract Him. Jesus knew the journey would be long and the road would be hard, but He went on His way.

So He could become our Way.

———————

reflection 5

DROP YOUR NETS

"At once they left their nets and followed him."

Matthew 4:20

Related Scripture
Matthew 4:18-22

Gentle waves slipped ashore
and sifted sand through a mountain of nets.

A screeching tern, perched high on an oar,
peered into the empty boat.

And the footprints pointed away.

They were men with a mission. "Catch fish. Sell fish. Sleep a bit. Eat a bite. Do it again." And they did. Day after day. Year after year. Until Jesus walked by with the words, *"Come, follow me."* More compelling than a command, the invitation offered grand prospects but demanded a great price—themselves.

"Come." He met them where they were, but they had to choose to move—away from their security, out of their comfort zone, into His mission.

"Follow." Not arriving as one who leads, but as one who would listen, who would learn, who would closely follow the footsteps of the Master.

"Me." And therein lay the biggest challenge of the call. In those days, many rabbis garnered disciples. Peter and Andrew noticed them at the Temple. James and John could spot them on the street. But which rabbi was right? Which teacher told the truth? Which master marked the way to God that could and should be trusted? Others might guess, but they knew.

"At once, they left their nets and followed him." They walked away from the good and came to God. Not sure of the "what" but certain of the "Who." Not joining a cause but joining with Christ.

They held on to nothing and ran to Him with everything.

Drop your nets.
Answer the call.

---

6 *reflection 6*

NO CORKSCREW NEEDED

"You have saved the best till now."

John 2:10

Related Scripture
John 2:1-11

Perhaps they underestimated the crowd. Or at least the crowd's consumption. Either way, the glasses were empty, and the groom was embarrassed. At Jewish weddings, as long as there was wine, all was well, but that afternoon in Cana, unfilled containers were causing a crisis.

Mary noticed the dilemma and wanted Jesus to help. Though she could do nothing, she knew He could do everything. His mother had no doubt Jesus was divine (His virgin birth had been plenty of proof), but the disciples with Him were relying more on words than works. Andrew had believed the words of John the Baptist. Peter had believed his brother, and Nathanael had believed Philip, his friend.

Jesus had not yet performed any miracles, for this was only the third day of His public ministry. Perhaps He hadn't planned to prove His identity quite so soon—*"My time is not yet come,"* He said to His mom, but this feast faux pas did provide the perfect opportunity to begin.

So Jesus gave the word, and six stone jars became sacred carafes. Water in. Wine out. Transformed from mediocre to magnificent at the command of His will. "I'm confused," the banquet master marveled as he tasted the new brew. "Usually the finest wine is served first while the senses are still sharp, but you've saved the best till last."

The celebrating crowd didn't catch the miracle, but the few who needed to know knew. Jesus never intended to steal the show. He did what He did to build the belief of His boys. *"He thus revealed his glory, and his disciples put their faith in him."*

With glasses overflowing, the guests resumed their revelry, the servants stared in wonder, and the disciples toasted in trust.

God's glory glowed through a bunch of squished grapes, and the bouquet was unmistakable.

Vintage Jesus Circa 30 AD

7 reflection 7

THE MOUNTAIN PREACHER

"Now when he saw the crowds, he went up
on a mountainside and sat down…and he
began to teach them."

Matthew 5:1-2

Related Scripture
Matthew 5:1-7:29

He began with the benediction—heaping blessings upon the meek and merciful, the poor and the pure, the peacemakers and the persecuted. Then He continued, "You're like salt, so season. You're like light, so shine. God is praised most when you live best."

"I'm not here to abolish God's Law; I'm here to accomplish it, and His Law is deeper than you think. The Law says, 'Don't murder.' I say, 'Don't be menacing.' The Law says, 'Don't live out your lust.' I say, 'Don't look around with lust.'"

"A piece of paper isn't justification for divorce. Stay married unless someone is messing around. Otherwise everyone ends up in a mess."

"Say what you mean and mean what you say."

"Don't settle scores. Get the upper hand by giving."

"Don't only love the ones who love you. How does that show God? Have a heart for those who hate you, and be faultless like your Heavenly Father."

"Give quietly. Pray privately. Forgive frequently. Fast secretly."

"Your money might not be where your mouth is, but it shows where your heart is. Set your focus—and your funds—in heaven."

"Don't sweat the small stuff. Or the big stuff. Fretting can't alter anything, and your Father knows everything. Put Him first and all else will fall into place."

"Be careful with criticism. The standards you set for others will be used on you."

"Ask like you want something. Seek like you've lost something. Knock like you need something. God is good at giving good gifts."

"To sum it up in a sentence, treat others like you like to be treated."

"And watch your path. The wide way isn't the right way. Many people look good but live bad, and just because they know My name doesn't mean they know Me."

The discourse ended with an admonition, not an invitation. "The winds of the world never destroy those who pay attention and take action, but the storms of life demolish the one who hears yet fails to heed."

No organ played and no offering was taken, but the service was over. The Preacher moved from His mountain pulpit, and the congregation headed for home.

Sunday's way past, but we're still talking 'bout that sermon.
Must have been a good one.

———————————

reflection 8

THE VERDICT

"This is the verdict: Light has come into the world, but men loved darkness instead of light."

John 3:19

Related Scripture
John 3:1-21

S hrouded for secrecy, Nicodemus slipped through the streets into the darkened doorway. Perhaps he shouldn't have come, but he had. He had to. There was just something about Jesus. His aura of authenticity and authority seemed heavenly, but Jesus couldn't really be divine, could He? The question captivated Nicodemus's mind and compelled his nighttime mission.

Not sure where to start, he defaulted to the usual Pharisaical flattery. *"Rabbi, we know you are a teacher who has come from God. For no one could perform the miraculous signs you are doing if God were not with him."*

Jesus cut through the fluff and went straight to the facts. *"No one can see the kingdom of God unless he is born again."*

"Born again? How?" Nicodemus wondered—thinking biology not theology.

"Simple," Jesus replied. "Your mother brought you into this world. God's Spirit brings you into His."

"But how?" the confused man queried.

"You teach others, but you don't understand this yourself?" Jesus responded. "Then let Me explain. I'm here because God loved. I'm here because God gave. God didn't send Me to put the world down. He sent Me to make the world right. Belief in Me equals salvation. Unbelief equals condemnation."

Nicodemus shuffled in his seat and tried to process what he was hearing.

"This is the verdict," Jesus continued, and Nicodemus leaned closer. He knew all about verdicts. As a member of the Sanhedrin, the Jewish ruling council, he spent his days assessing cases and announcing outcomes. A verdict fused all the information into one final proclamation.

"This is the verdict," Jesus declared. *"Light has come into the world but men loved darkness instead of light.... Whoever lives by the truth comes into the light."*

The conversation was over.

After a verdict is read, nothing is left to be said. So Nicodemus stood to go.

He came as a plaintiff, planning to put truth on trial. He left as a defendant, guilty with no good arguments.

Jesus stood at the doorway and watched Nicodemus disappear into the darkness.

He had not come to this world to press charges.
He had come to offer pardons.
And the Judge Himself would pay the fine.

reflection 9

SHAME AND PREJUDICE

"Now he had to go through Samaria."

John 4:4

Related Scripture
John 4:1-42

E veryone in town knew her—or at least knew about her. Maybe that's why she came to the well at noon. The hot sun burned less than harsh stares. She brought only her jug, nothing more and no one else. She needed water. And some solitude.

But she would have none today for a man was sitting by the well. *What is he doing here?* she surely thought.

The disciples had wondered the same as they traveled into town. *"Now He had to go through Samaria,"* John records, and his irritation at Jesus' insistence resounds in his words. Most Jews took the long way around. What were a few (or many) more steps if one could avoid those sorry Samaritans? But the Master had mapped out the shortest course, not the most prejudiced path.

Knowing that those He would meet needed His love and that those He was with needed a lesson, Jesus had headed straight north.

Weary from the journey, He now rested by the well as the disciples went to grab some grub. Perhaps they felt Jesus should go shop since this was all His idea, but we hear no objection and we see only obedience. They went to find food. The woman came to fetch water. God was working in both.

"Will you give Me a drink?" Jesus kindly requested. The woman was surprised by what He asked and then startled by what He said. "You really should be asking Me for water. Mine satisfies thirst and stops it, too. Why don't you call your husband, and we'll continue our conversation?" When the woman said she was single, Jesus countered, "At least you're honest, but you've said 'I do' five times, and your current live-in isn't legal."

Sensing this guy was not your average well-wisher, the woman inquired about the proper place of worship. "You're caught up in the *where*," Jesus told her, "but God is concerned with the *how*." Wistfully she responded, "When Messiah comes, I'll finally understand." Jesus smiled and said, ""You're talking to the One you've been waiting for."

The woman ditched her jug and dashed into town to testify.

The disciples returned and found Jesus already full. The best lunch special is the Lord's work.

Jesus stayed in Sychar for two more days. The disciples learned about the Samaritans, and the Samaritans learned about salvation.

God's agenda is sometimes not ours.
Often it amazes us. Occasionally it aggravates us.
Don't object. Obey.

People around you are thirsty.
Share the water.

———————————

10 *reflection 10*

THE FUNERAL CRASHER

"Then he went up and touched the coffin....
The dead man sat up and began to talk."

Luke 7:14-15

Related Scripture
Luke 7:11-17

I wondered why everyone going my way traveled so slowly. The two-lane country road seemed a bit narrow yet not unusually so. Clouds sprinkled showers, but the weather wasn't stormy. As pavement wound by field and forest, I carefully but casually weaved around several cars whose lights were also shining brightly for safety. Then I saw the hearse.

The long, black wagon mournfully turned toward the graveyard gate, and I was mortified. How rude. How uncouth. How disrespectful. Sensing no good means to make up for my bad manners, I sheepishly (and slowly) drove past the entrance as my exit. I felt like a funeral crasher.

But I wasn't the first.

"As [Jesus] approached the town gate, a dead person was being carried out—the only son of his mother, and she was a widow…. When the Lord saw her…he said, 'Don't cry.' Then he went up and touched the coffin."

The boy was dead. The mom was devastated. And friends could do nothing but go with her to the grave-yard. But Jesus, disregarding the rules of society and the restrictions of religion, stepped into the sorrow, told the mom not to cry, and touched the coffin. How callous and how unclean, for her tears were on-target and the casket off-limits. But all the crying soon became confetti as Jesus revived the corpse and returned the lad to his mom.

For my interment indiscretion, I could only offer apologies, but when Jesus crashed a funeral, He caused a fiesta!

And the party goes on. *"You were dead in your trans-gressions and sins…. But because of his great love for us, God, who is rich in mercy, made us alive with Christ"* (Ephesians 2:1,4).

Our celebration starts in the cemetery.
Don't be stiff. Sit up and begin to talk.
"God has come to help his people."

---

11 *reflection 11*

STORM STORIES

"But when [Peter] saw the wind, he was
afraid and, beginning to sink, cried out,
'Lord, save me!'"

Matthew 14:30

Related Scripture
Matthew 14:22-33

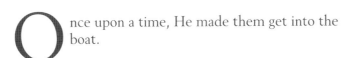

Once upon a time, He made them get into the boat.

The disciples were reluctant to leave without Him, but Jesus insisted they embark alone. While they paddled, He stayed and prayed. Somewhere along their way, the breeze began to blow—hard. Rough water made for tough rowing, and they were going nowhere fast. From the mountainside, Jesus watched and waited. Finally, in the darkness before dawn, He stepped into their storm and started across the sea, walking on the water.

"It's a ghost!" they screamed when they saw Him, but Jesus called back, *"It's me. Don't be afraid."*

Peter stopped the speculation with a request, *"Lord, if it's you…tell me to come to you."*

"Come ahead," Jesus commanded.

With faithful feet, Peter moved from the safety of the boat to the spray of the waves, but the howling wind which thrashed his cloak soon shook his confidence. As his focus shifted from the Savior to the circumstances, he began to sink.

"Lord, save me!" Peter shouted as he slipped into the deep. One strong grip later, the two of them headed back to the boat. As Jesus climbed in, the winds went away, and the disciples were in awe.

THE END…But not really.

We've all been terrified in tempests. We all struggle in squalls. God is not watching from a distance but instead goes with us through the gale. Sometimes He calms the storm. Sometimes He calms the sailor.

Don't stop believing. The water can handle your weight. But if you do start to sink, pull a Peter. Cry out to Jesus, and He will save you.

Swallow your pride and not the sea.
The Lifeguard is always on duty.

———————————————

12 *reflection 12*

THE BIG QUESTION

"'But what about you?' he asked. 'Who do you say I am?'"

Matthew 16:15

Related Scripture
Matthew 16:13-16

T hey knew He would eventually pop the question. But this time, the one answering was more nervous than the One asking.

Jesus waited until they traveled to Caesarea Philippi. Once the center of Baal worship, the city now boasted mountainside shrines for the Greek god Pan and a temple honoring Augustus Caesar. Against this backdrop of assorted belief, Jesus inquired, *"Who do people say the Son of Man is?"* The disciples replied, *"Some say John the Baptist; others say Elijah; and still others, Jeremiah or one of the prophets."*

Not a bad crowd to hang with. John the Baptist preached from his heart but lost his head. Elijah called fire from heaven and was caught up in fire to heaven. Jeremiah's passion flowed through his weeping and his warnings.

Many other prophets repeated God's plea for repentance and His promise of rescue. Good men. God's men. But none were God.

The common crowd held Jesus in high regard—but not high enough. Their estimations were respectful but wrong. Admirable but incorrect. Nice but no.

However, Jesus' first question was really just a setup for His second. *"'But what about you?' he asked. 'Who do you say I am?'"* He didn't wish for public opinion; He wanted their personal conviction.

Peter spoke first, *"You are the Christ, the Son of the living God."* The Christ. The Messiah. The Savior. The One sent from God Himself to bring us to Himself. Not just a do-gooder but divine.

Only two choices describe Peter's statement—Total Truth or Tall Tale. There can be no middle ground. The word on the street doesn't matter. Our words of belief do.

Who do you say He is?
Your answer should ring with commitment.
(And by the way, kneeling would be appropriate.)

---

13 *reflection 13*

KEEP THE CHANGE

"As he was praying, the appearance of his face changed, and his clothes became as bright as a flash of lightning."

Luke 9:29

Related Scripture
Luke 9:28-36

T hey say, "Prayer changes things," but no one expected this.

One day, *"[Jesus] took Peter, John and James with him and went up onto a mountain to pray."* Made sense to them. On a hill, the Father seemed closer, the weather cooler, the noise quieter. And their eyes sleepier.

But this time as Jesus prayed, His face began to glow, and soon His whole being was bright with God's glory.

Glory Jesus abdicated for His arrival on earth.
Glory He deserved but had deferred.
Glory He gave up so He could give to us.

For several minutes on the mountain, Jesus was what He had been and what He would become.

Moses and Elijah, also shining in splendor, took a time-out from Paradise to talk with Jesus about the upcoming cross. Startled by such sights, the disciples' drowsiness quickly disappeared, and they *"became fully awake."*

Peter found his voice and wanted to stay on the mount. God used His voice and wanted Peter to shut his mouth.

And then it was over. The extraordinary faded to the usual, and only the four of them remained. But the glimpse of God's glory would never go away. Throughout the coming years, this "there's more to life than meets the eye" moment motivated their message and inspired their endurance.

Wake up! And listen up! God still speaks, and He still shines. In the midst of the mundane, He delights to give us glimpses of His glory.

Just pray with your eyes open.

---

14 *reflection 14*

DROP THE ROCKS

"If any of you is without sin, let him be the
first to throw a stone at her."

John 8:7

Related Scripture
John 8:1-11

With outward disdain but inner delight, the Pharisees thrust the woman in front of Jesus. One glance and you knew she was guilty. Her face was flushed with shame and frozen in fear. Her trembling hands clutched her clothes as she awaited her fate in terror.

"Teacher, this woman was caught in the act of adultery. In the Law Moses commanded us to stone such women. Now what do you say?" The men stepped back smugly—licking their chops. The trap was laid perfectly. An answer either way would snare Him, and then they could seize Him.

But Jesus didn't bite the bait. *"Jesus bent down and started to write on the ground with his finger."*

"I said, 'What do You say we do with her, Teacher?' We know what Moses said, but You tell us what to do."

They didn't care about her. Or God's holiness. They just wanted Him. So Jesus straightened up and straightened them out. *"When they kept on questioning him, he straightened up and said to them, 'If any one of you is without sin, let him be the first to throw a stone.'"* Jesus didn't give them an answer; He gave them an ultimatum. "If you've never lusted, line up and fire away."

The old geezers left first. And quickly. Probably not so much from conviction as from concern that Jesus might start pointing fingers and naming names. The young and eager hung around a bit longer—initially convinced they could still capture their prey but finally forced away by their own failures. The ones trying to get the dirt on Jesus left brushing it off themselves, and all the while, Jesus kept writing on the ground.

It was just the two of them now. The guilty and the Guiltless. The harlot and the Holy One. The adulteress and the Almighty. He could throw every stone and be totally just. He could hurl all the rocks and be perfectly righteous. But He never even had one in His hand.

"Woman, where are they? Has no one condemned you?"

"'No one, sir,' she said."

"'Then neither do I condemn you,' Jesus declared."

He didn't ignore her sin; He acknowledged it, but He gave her a chance to walk away—away from their wrath and away from her wrong. *"Go now and leave your life of sin."*

We rarely sling stones for the right reasons.
Drop your rocks.

Or better yet, be like Jesus and never even pick one up.

———————————

THE ULTIMATE INFOMERCIAL

"One thing I do know. I was blind but now
I see!"

John 9:25

Related Scripture
John 9:1-38

A butterfly flitted past his nose, but he never even knew. A mangy dog darted into the path, but the man only heard growling. He endured the sun's heat but didn't enjoy its light. He felt love but couldn't picture a smile. Blind since birth, he could not see and he would not see.

No one believed it was for nothing. Surely unholiness caused this handicap. "Who sinned?" the disciples asked. "This man or his parents?"

"This affliction isn't to show what someone did wrong," Jesus answered. "It's to show what God can do right." He spit in the dirt, made some mud, and spread the mixture on the man's eyes. *"Go...wash in the Pool of Siloam,"* Jesus instructed.

The man went as he had gone before—by feeling the stones and counting the steps. His honed ears were open to hear obstacles. His flailing hands hoped to find any hindrances. Finally he arrived.

A splash at Siloam was all it took. The water washed away the mud and his malady. Bright light seemed to nearly blind him again. How bold! How beautiful! How glorious the shapes! How crazy the colors! The blue of the sky. The green of the trees. So that's what they meant by red! And who would have thought a donkey would be gray?

With a hoot and a holler he hurried home. The neighbors could hardly believe their eyes. "It's really me!" he assured them. "I went and washed, and now I see!" The Pharisees caught word of the wonder and stepped in to have their say. They asked for an explanation, and the ex-blind man answered, "I went and washed, and now I see." He couldn't look at the Lord, but he had heard His voice, felt His touch, and believed His word. His sight was living proof of God's power.

Not sure of the story, the Pharisees polled his parents, who stuck by their own son but wouldn't stand up for God's. The Pharisees then demanded the man admit Jesus was a sinner, but instead he declared, "I can't tell you much about the man, but I can tell you about the miracle. One thing I do know. I was blind but now I see!"

Infuriated by his comebacks and by his confidence that the One who healed had come from God, they banned the man from the synagogue. After they kicked him out, Jesus looked him up. He opened the man's heart just as He had opened his eyes. Once more the man could say, *"One thing I do know. I was blind but now I see!"*

We can testify to the same. We've never seen Jesus with our eyes, but we have heard His voice, felt His touch, believed His Word. Our lives are living proof of God's power. People will watch and people will wonder. They will question in amazement or quiz in anger.

Lifting Him up will do more than a lecture.
Stop explaining. Start exclaiming.
"One thing I do know. I was blind but now I see!"

---

16 reflection 16

THE LAME LEPERS

"Jesus asked, 'Were not all ten cleansed?
Where are the other nine?'"

Luke 17:17

Related Scripture
Luke 17:11-19

Mama might not have taught them, but somehow that's doubtful. Their plea of "Please" had landed them a miracle, but since they left without a "Thank you," the story seems incomplete.

"As [Jesus] was going into a village, ten men who had leprosy met him." The dreaded disease of leprosy rotted flesh and ruined lives. When leprosy appeared, the afflicted disappeared, immediately forced to leave all they loved and all they loved to do. Relocated outside of town, far from family and friends, they were required to tear their clothes, uncover their heads, and continually call, "Unclean! Unclean!" as a caution to those who might come too close. Except for this declaration of defilement, lepers were to be silent, not allowed to greet or return the greeting of any who passed by.

Lonely and alone, surviving until succumbing, they were desolate and desperate. Full of pain and loss. Empty of love and touch.

When the lepers spotted Jesus strolling down the road, hope stirred their helplessness. Tossing away caution and command, they cried out, *"Jesus, Master, have pity on us."* He did and directed them to the priest, whose official word of healing got you back into life like a doctor's note gets you back into school.

The lepers heard what Jesus said. They did what Jesus said. *"And as they went, they were cleansed."* Compliant steps led to clean skin. Their disease was gone. Their disdain was gone. Their despair was gone. In amazement, nine of them said, "Wow! Look at us!" but only one of them said, "Whoa! Look at Him!" *"One of them, when he saw he was healed, came back, praising God in a loud voice. He threw himself at Jesus' feet and thanked him."*

Ten said, "Please!" but only one said, "Thank you!"

"Please" and "Thank you." God knows they should go together. *"Jesus asked, 'Were not all ten cleansed? Where are the other nine?'"* He wasn't wondering about location but was asking about appreciation, and He never got an answer. Overjoyed in their healing, the lepers overlooked the Healer. They focused on the gift and forgot the Giver. How lame.

But on the one who returned to say thanks, extra blessings were bestowed. *"Rise and go,"* Jesus said. *"Your faith has made you well."* Not just cleansed but changed. More than restored skin, he received a rescued soul. Ten men went away that day with healed bodies, but one left with a whole heart. He politely asked for a gift, and when Jesus answered, the man cherished both the present and its Provider.

Request with graciousness and respond with gratitude. Don't be like the lame lepers. Complete the story.

Put your "Please" and "Thank you" together, and you'll make more than just your mama happy!

———————————

17 *reflection 17*

A SHORT STORY

"Zacchaeus, come down immediately. I must stay at your house today."

Luke 19:5

Related Scripture
Luke 19:1-10

Zacchaeus was a wee little man—in many ways. His legs were short. His conscience small. His scruples scrawny. His name meant "righteous one," but Zacchaeus made his living the wrong way. He sold his loyalty to the Romans, collecting taxes for their country while charging extra to his countrymen. Zacchaeus was no puny employee of the Roman Revenue Service, and as a chief tax collector, his pockets were padded by those under his oversight. He found great pleasure in the power (and the profits) of his high position and felt that its big status compensated for his small stature.

But no VIP seating was provided the day Jesus entered Jericho, and as push came to shove, Zacchaeus found himself in the back of the pack. He couldn't see over the crowd. He wasn't able to see through the crowd. And Zacchaeus wanted to see Jesus.

"So he ran ahead and climbed a sycamore-fig tree to see him, since Jesus was coming that way." Running and climbing were both improper actions for an important official, but Zacchaeus didn't care. He desired to at least catch a glimpse, for he never dared to dream this man might be his guest. But much to his surprise, Jesus stopped at the sycamore, looked up, went out on a limb, and invited Himself over for dinner. While the crowd muttered about His dining place, Zacchaeus marveled at His divine grace.

Zacchaeus stood up and stood tall as he said, "Look, Lord, I'm giving away half of what I have. And the cheap money I've made by cheating, I'll pay back four times over."

Jesus replied, "Salvation has found a home in this house today, for this man is now part of the family of faith. The Son of Man came to seek and to save the ones who are lost."

Zacchaeus lived up to his name.
Jesus lived out His mission.
That's the long—and short—of it.

———————————

18 *reflection 18*

HOSANNA!

"Hosanna! Blessed is he who comes in the name of the Lord!"

Mark 11:9

Related Scriptures
Matthew 21:1-11
Luke 19:28-40

The three years of Jesus' ministry had passed quickly. The days had been filled with hungry crowds. *"The number of those who ate was about five thousand men, besides women and children."* Heartfelt confessions. *"You are the Christ, the Son of the living God."* Late night questions. *"Rabbi, how can a man be born when he is old?"* And daytime confrontations. *"If any one of you is without sin, let him be the first to throw a stone."* The disciples had feasted and followed. They had listened and loved. They had stuck around when others walked away. And now it was time to celebrate again.

Jerusalem was always packed during Passover week. Since this year was no different, they spent the night in Bethany. The crowds there were small, and the company of Mary, Martha, and Lazarus was sweet.

As the Sabbath ended and Sunday began, they headed toward Jerusalem. Jesus told two of them, "Go into the next village and bring back the donkey you find tied there. If anyone asks what you are doing, just say, 'The Lord needs it.'" Jesus needs a donkey? Jesus didn't ride donkeys. He walked.

But they obeyed and brought the donkey. Jesus climbed on as though He belonged and began to trot toward town. Word spread fast that He was on His way. Some spread their cloaks in the road while others cut and waved palm branches. All began to cry out, "Hosanna! Hosanna to the Son of David! Hosanna in the Highest! Blessed is He who comes in the name of the Lord! Hosanna! Save us!"

The bellows of praise rose above the bustle of the day. The haughty-but-not-holy religious leaders showed up and tried to rain on the parade, but Jesus countered their request for silence with the reply, "If the people don't shout, the rocks will scream."

"When Jesus entered Jerusalem, the whole city was stirred and asked, 'Who is this?' The crowds answered, 'This is Jesus.'"

Something in them knew this man was their hope. Somehow they felt He had come to help. The exclamations burst from their hearts and poured through their lips, for they couldn't keep quiet.

And we shouldn't.

May the world always hear our *"Hosanna!"*

———————————

19 *reflection 19*

MISSING GOD

"If you, even you, had only known on this day what would bring you peace."

Luke 19:42

Related Scripture
Luke 19:41-48; 21:1-4

I t was the final week of His life, and though no one else knew, Jesus did. He entered Jerusalem to cries of praise but paused and wept as He looked around. He could see the coming devastation and destruction of the city, and He knew the reason. *"Because you did not recognize the time of God's coming to you."*

God had come, and they had missed Him. The ones singing *"Hosanna!"* on Sunday would scream *"Crucify!"* on Friday. He had taught them. He had healed them. He had fed them. A few had received, but most had rejected. They had missed God.

Sorrow shifted to action when Jesus reached the Temple. For fifty years, Herod had been directing a massive remodel, and the building was now big, bold, and beautiful. Its shining stone and sturdy structure were a source of pride for all Judea. Thousands thronged the Temple during Passover week. Many were foreigners who needed to exchange currency. Some were locals who swapped cash and sold sacrifices—for a "small" fee. Others were merchants simply using the Temple's terrace as a shortcut across town. Why carry your wares all the way around the hill when you could traipse right through the Temple courts?

Neither the chaos nor the crowds bothered Jesus, but the shady trading did. The dishonest charges and disregard for the holy were too much to take, so Jesus took charge. He flipped over the exchange tables, sending the coins and their crooked owners scrambling. He dumped the benches of the dove dealers. The birds flew and the bad guys fled. He closed the Temple thoroughfare, and the hawkers headed back down the mountain. "My house is a place to pray, not a place to pilfer," He demanded. They had missed God.

The next afternoon Jesus sat across from the Temple treasury and watched. Many gave much, their coins loudly clanging in the coffer. A poor widow walked by and dropped in two bits of copper. Although the small clink could barely be heard, the sound of her sacrifice rang loudly. "She put in more than all the rest," He said.

"The others, in their prosperity, only gave a tiny portion. She, in her poverty, gave her all—everything she had." She had not missed Him.

May we not, either.

In the midst of life's activities, opportunities, and abundance, may we not miss the only One who matters.

Even for a day.

20 *reflection 20*

THE SCENT OF SACRIFICE

"She broke the jar and poured the perfume."

Mark 14:3

Related Scripture
John 12:1-8

S	he gave all she had. All she had gathered from the past. All she had garnered for the future. Bound in a box of stone, the pint of perfume was worth at least a year's wages.

But on that evening in Bethany, Mary surrendered her savings and her security when she opened the jar and anointed Jesus. Passion compelled her present for she hoped to honor and she wanted to worship. Adoration flowed from the alabaster as the fragrance filled the room.

Some with Him were appalled. "What a waste!" they accused. "Such large treasure could have done much good. She should have helped out the poor instead of pouring out the perfume."

The rebuke from Jesus came quickly and sternly. "Leave her alone. She did something beautiful. She prepared My body for burial. The needy aren't going anywhere, but I am. And for the record, from now on, her story will be spread everywhere My story is shared."

The last drops fell from His feet to the floor. The box lay broken, but the aroma lingered in the air. Her gift was expensive. And priceless. It was extravagant. And precious.

We will never give more than He is worth.
Nothing smells sweeter than the scent of sacrifice.

———————————

HOW JESUS LOVED

LOVE
BEYOND
DEGREE

reflection 21

KEEP THE FESTIVAL

"For Christ, our Passover lamb, has been sacrificed. Therefore let us keep the Festival."

1 Corinthians 5:7-8

Related Scripture
Luke 22:7-13

"Busy" best described Jerusalem on Passover Thursday. Mom cleaned meticulously, removing every speck of yeast from the home. Dad inspected thoroughly, confirming all was spotless. Kids waited and wanted—since fasting until supper was the usual practice. All day long a sense of expectation filled the air.

Jesus eagerly desired to celebrate this special evening with His disciples, so He summoned Peter and John. *"Go and make preparations for us to eat the Passover... As you enter the city, a man carrying a jar of water will meet you. Follow him [home]...and say to the owner of the house, 'The Teacher asks: Where is the guest room, where I may eat the Passover with my disciples?' He will show you a large upper room, all furnished. Make preparations there."*

"All furnished." The table was provided, as were the wine, unleavened bread, and paste of bitter herbs. What had the homeowner been thinking as he arranged the upper room? He knew he was preparing for something or someone, but I would guess he never guessed the Lord Himself would come calling.

He still comes calling. He summons us each morning and says, "Go. I've been ahead of you and provided everything for you. Get ready. Today is a celebration, a special time of remembering God's grace and giving thanks. I desire to spend this day with you."

Peter and John didn't have to set the table. They just needed to bring the lamb.
We don't need to bring a sacrifice. We just need to bring ourselves.

The Lamb has been provided.
And He has furnished all we need.

---

22 *reflection 22*

NO SELF-SERVICE

"I have set you an example that you should
do as I have done for you."

John 13:15

Related Scripture
John 13:1-17

I t was time to eat, and though no one was shout-
ing, "Wash up!" they all knew they should. Dusty
dirt from the Mount Olive road had left their feet
grimy and soiled, but since the host hadn't sent a servant, they reclined around the table and began.

Then Jesus *"got up from the meal, took off his outer cloth-
ing, and wrapped a towel around His waist."* Surely He
wasn't. Not Him. No way. Anybody but Him. They all
knew they should have, but none of them had. Their
noisy chatter fell into awkward silence. What could they
say? What should they say?

Finally, Peter could stand it no longer. *"Lord, are you
going to wash my feet? You shall never wash my feet."*

Jesus gently responded, *"Peter, you do not realize now
what I am doing, but later you will understand."*

"[Jesus] poured water into a basin and began to wash his disciples' feet, drying them with the towel that was wrapped around him."

He washed the feet of the one who would turn Him in. He washed the feet of the ones who would turn and run. Tenderly and thoroughly, He washed them all.

"When he had finished…he put on his clothes and re-turned to his place." Some stared at the ground. Some stared at Jesus. His own gaze moved around the table.

"You call me 'Teacher' and 'Lord,' and rightly so, for that is what I am. Now that I, your Lord and Teacher, have washed your feet, you should also wash one an-other's feet."

The Beautiful One had washed the feet of His betrayer. The King of kings had washed the feet of His subjects.

He left us a great example.
He left us no good excuse.

---

reflection 23

THE BREAD AND THE CUP

"He took the bread, gave thanks and broke it, and gave it to them."

Luke 22:19

"He took the cup, gave thanks and offered it to them."

Mark 14:23

Related Scripture
Luke 22:14-20

E aster Sunday, 1978. As an eager eight-year-old, I rose early and dressed quickly for the sunrise service at the local golf course. Full of anticipation and excitement, I felt like a princess in my elegant, handed-down Easter outfit. I was trying so hard to stay prim and proper when somehow, during communion, I spilled grape juice on the front of my pretty, pink dress. The red pigment stained the fabric as the drops rolled down the bodice onto my sash.

It was an accident.
I didn't mean to do that.

"And [Jesus] said to them, 'I have eagerly desired to eat this Passover with you…. I will not eat it again until it finds fulfillment in the kingdom of God.' He took the bread, gave thanks…and gave it to them." "He took the cup, gave thanks, and offered it to them."

Since they could toddle and taste, the disciples had been partaking at Passover, remembering back to the grand night in Egypt when God had delivered His people and looking forward to the great day in Israel when He would do it again.

What did Jesus mean by *"This bread is my body"*? He held matzo bread. Its yeastless dough had been rolled flat and pierced. During the Passover ritual, a piece was broken, wrapped in a cloth, and set aside. *"This is my body which is broken for you."*

What did He mean by *"This cup is the new covenant in my blood, which is poured out for you"*? The disciples knew of God's covenant with Abraham and Moses. They had read the promises given to David and spoken through Daniel. But the priests still prayed and the lambs were still slain. A new covenant? Oh, to God that there would be one! And soon!

"Carrying his own cross, he went out to…Golgotha. Here they crucified him…. One of the soldiers pierced Jesus' side with a spear, bringing a sudden flow of blood."

The red pigment stained His flesh as the drops rolled down His body onto our sin.

It was no accident.
He meant to do that.

24

reflection 24

TOGETHER

"Do not let your hearts be troubled."

John 14:1

Related Scripture
John 14:1-27

"*Do not let your hearts be troubled.*" Nice to say now, but Jesus had just said, "One of you is going to betray Me. Peter, you will deny Me. And, by the way, I will be with you only a little longer." Why should their hearts *not* be troubled?

Because of what came next. *"Trust in God, trust also in me. In my Father's house are many rooms; if it were not so, I would have told you. I am going there to prepare a place for you. And if I go and prepare a place for you, I will come back and take you to be with me."*

Surely the disciples smiled. Some were married, and the rest hoped to be. They all knew the drill. You chose a girl and met with her dad. If he agreed, you drank a cup of wine to seal the deal, told the lucky lady you would see her later, and headed back home—to your father's house. There you prepared a place for the two of you, an extra room that would be just right. When all was ready, you went to get your bride and brought her back to be with you.

"I am going there to prepare a place for you." "I will come back and get you. You will be where I am."
We will be together.

But what about now? What will happen? Will we be left alone? Jesus could sense their anxious hearts and calmed them with His words. *"I will not leave you as orphans; I will come to you."* "My Father and I will come to you and make Our home with you."
We will be together.

In our eternity, we will be with Him.
In our every day, He will be with us.

Let not your heart be troubled.

———————————

25 *reflection 25*

THE VINE AND THE BRANCHES

"I am the vine; you are the branches."

John 15:5

Related Scripture
John 15:1-17

J esus talked as they walked from the upper room to the garden. Perhaps He paused as they passed a vineyard. *"I am the vine; you are the branches… and my Father is the gardener."* Even the ones who didn't grow grapes got it. Vineyards were plentiful in Palestine, and caretakers were continually busy trimming back the good, cutting off the bad, and gathering fruit in season.

Branches—and believers—are useless on their own. Connection to the Vine brings life and bears fruit. From Him come the nourishment you need and the refreshment you require. His strength supports you, and His love lifts you. You're held by His holiness and kept by His kindness.

You didn't sprout on your own. You were grafted by God's grace; so stay close. Abiding will lead to abundance.

Don't grow your own way. Let the Father prune you and place you. Pruning is painful but effective, producing quality over quantity. You might be scared of the shears, but your Father knows best what needs to stay and what must go.

And try not to whine about your whereabouts. You might not like your location, but it's where the Son will beam brightest and you will be sweetest. God positions His branches for optimum output, and since your fruit reflects His faithfulness, He grows you for His glory.

Proximity increases production, and clusters will come as you stay close. The results of your relationship will nourish others and bring the flavor of faith to their lives. Without Him you wither and are weak, but abiding in Christ brings bunches of blessings.

As they walked away, the vineyard looked the same. But they would never look at a vineyard the same.

Abide.

26 *reflection 26*

THE OTHER LORD'S PRAYER

"Father, the time has come. Glorify your
Son, that your Son may glorify you."

John 17:1

Related Scripture
John 17:1-26

He began with "Father." Not the inclusive "Our Father" of a congregation but the intimate "My Father" of a child. And then He continued—for quite a while. (The clock, not the content, is the reason we don't quote this one in church!) On the night before He died, between the teaching and the turmoil, Jesus paused to pray—for Himself, for His disciples, for you.

He didn't lower His head but looked to heaven and raised His requests. He asked the Father to restore the glory He had left there when He came here. Jesus was ready for its return.

He lifted up His disciples—those special few who trusted God's truth and would take it around the globe. His concern was their safety and their sanctification.

Jesus desired that they be set apart in the world, not that they separate from the world, so He asked for their protection from Satan and their purity from sin.

And Jesus prayed for us. The chain-reaction Christians. Those linked to His life through the handed-down but never-worn-out message of His love. He hoped our unity would display His divinity to a watching world, and He wanted us to be with Him.

His requests then ended, but God's reply goes on.

The Father exalted the Son. He guarded the disciples. Century after century, He has shown His power through His people. And one day we will be where He is, gazing on His glory and never going away.

God's answer will then be complete. And Jesus will add the final "Amen."

So be it.

———————————

27 *reflection 27*

GETHSEMANE

"Not my will, but yours be done."

Luke 22:42

Related Scripture
Matthew 26:36-46

The conflict, which had been simmering under the surface, erupted into full-scale war. Opposing forces battled with all their might, clashing and struggling to overcome. And the fate of billions hung in the balance. But someone walking through the quiet garden would have noticed only a kneeling Jesus and three dozing disciples.

Gethsemane. The word means "oil press." At the place where olives were crushed until their oil flowed, Jesus prayed until His sweat fell—as blood. Knowing the battle would be fierce, He instructed eight disciples to sit and wait while He brought Peter, James, and John along for comfort and support.

"Stay here and keep watch with me," He told them. Was it really too much to ask? Could they not hear the anguish in His voice as He said, *"My soul is overwhelmed*

with sorrow to the point of death"? Granted, they had satisfied stomachs, sleepy eyes, and sad hearts, but Jesus needed them. Jesus was distressed. Jesus was disturbed. Jesus was struggling.

All God? Yes. All man? That, too. Not a combination of the best of both, but every bit of both resided in the desperate figure who fell to the ground and cried out, *"Father, everything is possible for you." "If you are willing, take this cup from me; yet not my will, but yours be done."*

He fought and He won. Submission is always the biggest battle. God's will versus our wants. God's design versus our desires. As you struggle to obey, remember that He has been there. And He won.

All the while, His special friends, His closest companions on earth, couldn't stay awake and watch. As they snoozed, He surrendered.

They lost the battle, but He won the war.
And in His victory, we are more than conquerors.

---

28 *reflection 28*

HANDING JESUS OVER AND OUT

"Judas...asked, 'What are you willing to give me if I hand him over to you?'"

Matthew 26:14-15

Related Scripture
Matthew 26:14-15,47-50
Matthew 27:1-5

The plot was planned for profit. Judas had followed Jesus for three years, enjoying the favors but not engaging the faith. He was the treasurer who couldn't be trusted, often helping himself to the money given to help others. But more was never enough, for one who craves cash can't be content.

Goaded by greed, Judas sought to betray God. After scoffing at Mary's sacrifice (and sulking from the loss of loot), he approached the chief priests and put out feelers for figures. *"What are you willing to give me if I hand him over to you?"* They counted out thirty coins. Silver coins. Enough money to redeem a slave or rat on a Savior. *"From then on Judas watched for an opportunity to hand him over."*

Time wasn't on his side until Passover Thursday when he let Jesus clean his feet but not change his heart. In the middle of the meal, Jesus handed Judas soaked bread and a shocking bid, *"What you are about to do, do quickly."* Realizing Jesus knew of his plans surely startled Judas but not enough to stop him. He led the soldiers to the garden and with a kiss to kill, faked his affection and fled.

When Jesus was condemned to death, a remorseful Judas, whose focus had been the income not the outcome, rushed to the religious leaders and pleaded, "I have sinned. This man has done nothing wrong, and I have done nothing right!" But the priests felt no pity for the distraught disciple and refused to change their charge. In torment, Judas slung the silver into the Temple and tied a noose around his neck.

Judas and Jesus died the same day.
Judas hung himself for his own sin.
Jesus let others hang Him for ours.

The bottom line is never big enough to justify betrayal.
Watch for opportunities to hand Jesus out.
Not hand Him over.

---

29 *reflection 29*

I AM

"'I am he,' Jesus said."

John 18:5

Related Scripture
John 18:1-9

The burning bush crackled in the air as Moses posed his question. *"Who am I, that I should go to Pharaoh and bring the Israelites out of Egypt?"* God's indirect answer of "I will be with you" didn't reassure his hesitant heart, so Moses tried again by asking, "Who are You?" *"Suppose I go to the Israelites...and they ask, 'What is his name?' Then what shall I tell them?"*

"God said to Moses, 'I AM WHO I AM.'...Say to [them], 'I AM has sent me to you.'"

I AM. The God who devastated Egypt and divided the Red Sea. I AM. The God who showered manna from heaven and squeezed water from a rock. I AM. The God who knocked down Jericho and knocked over

Goliath. I AM. The God who shut up Daniel's lions and opened up Peter's prison. I AM. The God who cried in Bethlehem's manger and celebrated at Cana's wedding.

I AM. The God who took the traitor's kiss and turned to the garden crowd. *"Who is it you want?"* He asked. The soldiers, officials, and Pharisees, carrying their torches, lanterns, and weapons, replied, *"Jesus of Nazareth."*

"I AM," Jesus said. And *"they drew back and fell to the ground."*

He could have struck them dead with His words. Instead, He knocked them down with His name. He let them get back up and lead Him away. He let them beat Him. He let them crucify Him.

Because He is I AM—the God who saves us.

He still is.
It should knock us to our knees.

---

30 *reflection 30*

THE PINK SLIP

"Those who had arrested Jesus took him to Caiaphas, the high priest."

Matthew 26:57

Related Scripture
Matthew 26:57-68

I t was his last day on the job, and he didn't even know it.

For fifteen years Caiaphas had traveled to the Temple to punch his time card, but he was never truly off-duty. As man's representative before God, he was earth's connection to heaven's perfection. He managed the observances, directed the worship, and supervised the sacrifices.

His position as high priest was one of importance and influence—both of which Caiaphas enjoyed. Both of which he felt were jeopardized by this Jesus of Nazareth who for the past three years had taught and testified about the coming of God and the Kingdom of God. The public gave Jesus the popularity Caiaphas craved.

Too much attention was paid to His works and too much authority was put in His words. Jealous of Jesus more than jealous for God, Caiaphas let the green-eyed monster turn him into one.

He tried to capture Jesus, to catch Him—in person, in practice, in preaching, but his attempts at arrest had been for naught. Until now. With some underhanded help, he had his man, and he had his plan.

The trial was ugly. Many false witnesses made charges, but their testimonies didn't match. Finally two came forward and accused, "This man said He could destroy the Temple and rebuild it in three days." Frustrated that Jesus didn't refute the findings, Caiaphas forced Him to speak by invoking the holy. *"I charge you under oath by the living God: Tell us if you are the Christ, the Son of God."* Silence had been the appropriate response to insolence and arrogance, but when asked specifically, Jesus answered with certainty. *"It is as you say…. In the future you will see the Son of Man sitting at the right hand of the Mighty One and coming on the clouds of heaven."*

The truth was more than Caiaphas could take. He tore his clothes and turned in the verdict. Guilty of blasphemy. Worthy of death.

Jesus would die to do God's will, but Caiaphas's name should never have been on the warrant. He ought to have understood atonement better than anyone in the business. Instead, he missed the biggest point of his job description.

As he called for Christ's crucifixion, Caiaphas signed his own pink slip. By the next afternoon earth's high priest would be succeeded by the heaven's Own, and Caiaphas's occupation would be obsolete. Stepping down should have been a delight, but sadly, he stayed in a dead-end job.

Jesus wasn't a threat. He was a promise.
Caiaphas should have crossed his heart—not his arms.
Then the cross would have done him some good.

STAND BY YOUR MAN

"Before the rooster crows, you will disown me three times!"

John 13:38

Related Scripture
Luke 22:54-62

Tshirts, license plates, and bumper stickers loudly proclaim our allegiances. We give generously and cheer passionately for the theme or team that holds our loyalty. But what if the losses outnumber the victories? What if the other party wins the election? What if the cure is not quickly found? Will we remain a fan, or will we walk away?

"Peter said to [Jesus], 'Even if everyone else deserts you, I never will.…Even if I have to die with you, I will never deny you.'" Peter was certain of his loyalty to the Lord, but Jesus knew better. *"Before the rooster crows, you will disown me three times!"*

Because the night was cold, Peter edged closer to the warm fire. He had followed at a distance as the soldiers led Jesus to the home of the high priest and was trying his best to blend with the courtyard crowd.

"You are not one of his disciples, are you?" asked a curious servant girl. *"I am not,"* Peter quickly replied and hurried toward the gateway. *"This fellow is one of them,"* another said. *"I am not!"* Peter adamantly responded, but the man kept insisting, *"Didn't I see you with him in the [garden]?" "Surely you are one of them." "[Peter] began to call down curses on himself, and he swore to them, 'I don't know this man you're talking about.'"*

His expletive was interrupted by a rooster's startling crow. *"The Lord turned and looked straight at Peter. Then Peter remembered the word the Lord had spoken to him…. And he went outside and wept bitterly."*

Peter knew. Jesus knew. Peter knew Jesus knew he had denied Him, he had rejected Him, he had disowned Him, and Peter wept. Hot tears of anguish poured from his eyes as he sobbed with sorrow and regret. Not sure what his allegiance to Jesus would cost him, Peter had been too scared to find out. Too chicken. No wonder a rooster crowed.

Jesus would forgive and Jesus would restore, for although Peter threw up his hands, Jesus never let go. He always stands by His man.

Don't cry foul. Be faithful.
Identifying with Jesus might bring some pain, but denying Him will hurt much more.

32 *reflection 32*

FENCES AND FAILURES

"What shall I do…with Jesus?"

Matthew 27:22

Related Scriptures
Matthew 27:11-26
John 18:28-19:16

As governor of Judea, Pontius Pilate was charged with three main duties—maintain order, enforce justice, and collect taxes. Although his kingdom was small, the possibility of problems loomed large as several cultures clashed within its narrow confines, and all seemed ready to revolt against Rome. Pilate's main residence was in Caesarea, but he moved to Jerusalem during religious festivals to keep down any trouble that might come up.

"He's a criminal! We want him dead!" the Pharisees shouted as they shoved Jesus into the royal palace. (Their laws barred them from entering such a heathen place during such a holy week.) "Are you a king?" Pilate asked the already battered and bruised Jesus. "Is that your own idea or are you simply repeating what you've heard?" Jesus questioned in reply.

"What is it you've done?" Pilate wanted to know. "I am a king," Jesus declared. *"For this reason I was born and... came into the world, to testify to the truth."*

This guy? A king? He was certainly not like other kings Pilate knew. He was not pompous or proud. He was not rich or renowned, but He did stand quietly, calmly, confidently—regally.

"Don't have anything to do with this innocent man," Pilate's wife warned as the insistent cries of *"Crucify Him!"* swelled into a raging chant. Pilate had to do something. Surely a cruel flogging would calm the bloodthirsty crowd.

The soldiers tied Jesus to a whipping post and nodded for the beating to begin. Leather, rocks, and metal ripped into His flesh and began to tear away His life. His blood and bits of His body splattered and scattered on the ground. He screamed. He convulsed. He writhed, as the torturous flails came again and again and again and again.

The soldiers jerked Jesus up and threw a purple robe around his mangled shoulders. "A crown for the king!" they mocked as they shoved the thorny spikes into His head. "Here's a scepter to rule us with. No, the better to rail You with!" they jeered while they struck Him furiously and spit in His face.

"Here is the man!" Pilate called to the crowd as Jesus came stumbling out in agony. *"Here is your king."* His voice begged approval from the mob, but, *"We have no king but Caesar,"* was their bawdy and blasphemous reply.

Innocence wasn't the issue. Pilate knew Jesus had done no wrong, but would Pilate do right? If he let Jesus go, he could lose control. He would lose respect. He might lose his throne. Was one life really worth the chaos? The crisis? The call from his Roman superior? "Don't go there," his wife had warned. *Don't go there*, his own heart cautioned. But…but…

You can't ride the fence forever. Indecision isn't an option. Eventually your choice, or lack of choosing, will cast your lot one way or the other. Pilate fell. And failed. But even as he tumbled, he tried to toss the blame. *"I am innocent of this man's blood,"* he declared as he washed his hands in front of the crowd.

Pilate maintained order, but he cast away justice. And his hands would never be clean.

Fences aren't for riding. They're for striding.
Land on His side.

---

33 *reflection 33*

GET OUT OF JAIL FREE

"He released Barabbas to them…and handed [Jesus] over to be crucified."

Matthew 27:26

Related Scripture
Matthew 27:15-26

Barabbas didn't know about Monopoly, but he knew about jail. And he wasn't just visiting. Insurrection and murder had landed him in the pen, and no roll of the dice or lucky card was going to get him out.

The door banged behind the heavy footsteps that approached his cell. His heart raced in horror. Would today be the day? He was surprised they had waited so long. Rome rarely dealt slowly with rebels.

Barabbas had seen terror in the faces of his victims. Did his own eyes now reflect the same fear? He had witnessed the agony of brutal executions. What would they do to him?

"Pilate says you're free." The gruff voice jolted his anxious thoughts. *Pilate. Oh, no.* Pilate was known for his cruelty, not his kindness. "I said, 'You're free!' You'd better get going before the crowd changes its mind."

The crowd! The feast! The governor's custom was to release one prisoner at the Passover feast, and Barabbas had been chosen! Chosen to live! His chains were loosed, and he was liberated.

But his freedom wasn't free. As Barabbas left the prison, Jesus was led to the cross.

Barabbas should have died, and Jesus should have lived. It wasn't a fair trade. But grace never is.

---

34 *reflection 34*

EMBRACE THE CROSS

"Above His head they placed the written
charge against Him."

Matthew 27:37

Related Scripture
John 19:17-22

Crucifixion was reserved for the worst of criminals. The agony and shame of a slow, torturous execution seemed fitting. The most evil in life deserved the most awful in death. The crimes of the guilty were attached to their crosses, serving notice to those around that similar choices would bring the same consequences.

"JESUS OF NAZARETH, THE KING OF THE JEWS." The indictment against Jesus was placed above His head. "Don't say he is the king of the Jews," the chief priests demanded of Pilate. "Instead, write that he says he is the king of the Jews." But Pilate resolutely responded, *"What I have written, I have written." "JESUS OF NAZARETH, THE KING OF THE JEWS."*

He died because of who He was, not because of what He had done. *"You are to give him the name Jesus,"* the angel informed Joseph many years before, *"because he will save his people from their sins."* He was born to die. That's why He came. And you are why He wanted to come.

Jesus was not a martyr. The cross was not a mistake. You could not be saved unless He suffered.

He died because of who He is—your Savior.
He died because of who you are—a sinner.
He died because *"God so loved the world that he gave his one and only Son, that whoever believes in him shall not perish but have eternal life."*

Embrace the cross.
It shows us who we are.
It shows us who He is.

Our worst brought out His best. And cost His life.
"To him belongs eternal praise!"

---

35 *reflection 35*

THE GOOD, THE BAD, AND THE UGLY

"Two other men, both criminals, were also led out with him to be executed."

Luke 23:32

Related Scripture
Luke 23:32-43

They were robbers. They had taken what wasn't theirs, and now the one thing they had was being taken away. As death drew near, both turned to the man in the middle. From the look of things, His day wasn't going any better than theirs. Maybe even worse. Being crucified was bad enough, but scornful taunts from priests and soldiers added extra agony.

One thief joined the jeering chorus. *"Aren't you the Christ? Save yourself and us!"* His mocking ridicule met quick rebuke from the other cross. *"Don't you fear God since you are under the same sentence? We are punished justly, for we are getting what our deeds deserve. But this man has done nothing wrong."*

How did he know? We don't know, but he knew. Perhaps he previously had heard of Jesus or maybe the events of the day simply showed him the truth. How he knew doesn't matter. What he did with what he knew does. *"Then he said, 'Jesus, remember me when you come into your kingdom.'"*

At that moment, on Calvary, the cross of earthly justice met the cross of heavenly grace. *"Jesus answered him, 'I tell you the truth. Today you will be with me in paradise.'"* The dying thief begged for mercy and was assured of a miracle. "As soon as this life ends, your new one begins—not just in a good place but in God's presence."

Jesus hung between two thieves.
One insulted in derision, "Forget about him. He's obviously no help."
The other implored in faith, "Remember me. You're my only hope."

The Redeemer remembered the robber.
The Redeemer remembers us.

And He will never forget.

36

DARKNESS IS DONE

"From the sixth hour until the ninth hour darkness came over all the land."

Matthew 27:45

Related Scripture
Luke 23:44-46

The Heavenly Father couldn't bear to look. In holiness and heartbreak, He turned His head. The sun stopped shining as the darkness of night covered the brightness of day. Perhaps God should have kept it light and forced us to view the awfulness of our sin, but the sacrifice was too sacred to be seen.

God's righteous justice demands payment for transgressions, and in those three agonizing hours, Jesus paid the eternal price for sin. *"The wages of sin is death,"* God decreed, and Jesus died our death. Much more than a state of nothingness or a circumstance of suffering, eternal death is No God, No Good, No Hope, Forever. We fail to grasp the terror of the thought or the horror of such reality, but Jesus did. For you. Forever.

The Father sacrificed His Son so we could be His children. The pain of the nails pales when compared to the penalty for our sin. The One who was all good became all bad—our bad—and in His anguish was abandoned by the Father. *"God made [Jesus], who had no sin, to be sin for us."* We do not understand the extent of His agony for we cannot comprehend the depth of our depravity, but Jesus did. For you. Forever.

Finally, it was over. The debt satisfied. The payment complete. *"It is finished!"* was His cry. A proclamation! A declaration! An exultation! *"The punishment that brought us peace was upon him and by his wounds we are healed"(Isaiah 53:5).*

Before the world was created, the cross was a reality. God knew what we would do. God knew what He would do, and He did it. For you. Forever.

"It is finished."
Our darkness has been dispelled, and the Son is shining brightly.

———————————

37 *reflection 37*

COME NEAR

"At that moment the curtain of the temple was torn in two from top to bottom."

Matthew 27:51

Related Scripture
Matthew 27:45-54

"D on't come near!" The flaming sword brandished by the angel at Eden's edge conveyed a solemn warning. Cast from the garden because of their sin, Adam and Eve could not return to God on their own.

"Don't come near!" Moses cautioned the desert-weary Israelites at the foot of Sinai. The mountain trembled along with the people as God descended in a fiery cloud. The consequence of crossing the boundary was immediate death. They could not come to God on their own.

"Don't come near!" God commanded the servants of His Temple. Only one person, once a year, could enter the inner room filled with God's presence. *"Tell [the high priest] not to come whenever he chooses into the Most Holy*

Place behind the curtain…or else he will die." Only on the Day of Atonement, only with the blood of the sin sacrifice in his hands, could the high priest come near. For no one dared to come to God on his own.

Passover Friday. Good Friday. Three o'clock in the afternoon. Time for the evening sacrifice. The priest began to make preparations, but the Father was already finished. *"When Jesus had cried out again in a loud voice, he gave up his spirit. At that moment the curtain of the temple was torn in two from top to bottom."*

"Come near!" God shouted as He reached down from heaven and ripped away the wall. No more barriers. No more blockades. No more set times or specific purposes. "Come near! Come now! Come close! The obstacle of sin has been obliterated. Jesus has paid it all. He has paved your way. Come, My children, come! You don't need a temple, an altar, or a priest. You just need to come!"

"Therefore, brothers, since we have confidence to enter the Most Holy Place by the blood of Jesus, by a new and living way opened for us through the curtain, that is, his body…let us draw near to God"(Hebrews 10:19-22).

We've been granted total access to the throne of God.
And our ID badge is shaped like a cross.

Come near.
Come now.

———————————

POMP AND CIRCUMSTANCE

"Taking Jesus' body, the two of them wrapped it, with the spices, in strips of linen."

John 19:40

Related Scriptures
John 19:38-42
Luke 23:50-54

S omebody had to do something with the body. The disciples had deserted. The women were weary. His brothers were absent, and His dad was dead.

The solution surfaced from an unlikely source. Stepping from the shadow of the Sanhedrin came Joseph of Arimathea and Nicodemus.

Joseph was wealthy, weak, and wise. As a secret disciple he had cowered in the corner, but now he boldly went public and asked Pilate for the body.

Since death by crucifixion was agonizingly slow, Pilate was surprised Jesus had passed so quickly. When his inquiry was met with affirmation, he granted the request.

Often Rome refused to release the corpses of those they considered rebels, but Pilate didn't want the responsibility—or the reminder.

Nicodemus met Joseph at the cross. Nicodemus had first approached Jesus in darkness, but here at last, he arrived in daylight. The two climbed up and took the body down. Bruised and bloody from the trauma of torture, it tumbled into their arms—lifeless and limp. Dead weight.

But, oh, how carefully they carried Him. How tenderly they touched Him. They wrapped His wounds in reverence and layered the burial spices with love. The strips of linen grave cloths were long like their sorrow and torn like their hearts.

The two worked quickly, for sundown signaled the Sabbath, and their mission must be accomplished before it began.

In the garden nearby was Joseph's own tomb—newly completed and never occupied. They laid the body on the stone ledge and rolled a rock across the entrance. They had done all they could do.

Their undertaking is inspiring. Driven by devotion not duty, they risked with no notion of reward.

They thought they were carrying Jesus to His grave—not His graduation.
But never has there been a more beautiful cap and gown.

———————————

39

reflection 39

SILENT SATURDAY

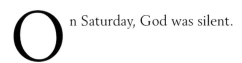

O n Saturday, God was silent.

Sandwiched between Friday's horror and Sunday's hallelujah is Saturday's silence. It was the Sabbath. A day of rest and rejoicing. A time for contemplation of what God had done and anticipation of what He would do. On Saturday, Jesus' followers could do neither. Rest would not come, for the reality was too raw. And in what could they rejoice?

The dream was dead. The final act finished, with the curtain closed forever. This was a true tragedy—ending with the funeral of the main character.

They were shocked and stunned. Jesus had called and they had come, certain He was the Savior. He spoke and the lame leaped. He touched and the blind could see. His word had healed desperate lepers and hailed a dead Lazarus. Couldn't He have done something? Anything?

On Saturday, the disciples weren't together. Safety might be in numbers, but crowds bring little comfort. Jesus had promised peace, but they were full of pain. He had assured them of abundance, but each felt empty. And all wondered, *Why?*

The ones who loved Him weren't waiting in hope. They were weeping. They didn't dream of a vacant grave. They were grieving. There was no expectation. No suspense. No "wait and see." Only silence. And the sound of heavy hearts breaking in anguish and sorrow.

We will never know the depth of their despair, for we will never spend a moment alive when Jesus is dead.

Saturday was silent, but the hush was holy. No one heard the rustling backstage as Jesus readied for His curtain call. They really should have known. Many times He had told them.

All's well that ends well.

reflection 40

ALIVE!

"He is not here; He has risen!"

Luke 24:6

Related Scripture
Luke 24:1-8

H e came back.

Back from the place all go, even if they don't want to. Back from the place none can leave, even if they do want to.

Jesus came back from death.

"He has risen!" The angel's astonishing proclamation startled the graveyard guests and sprinkled their heavy hearts with hope. *"Why do you look for the living among the dead? He is not here!"* He's alive! Jesus is alive! The silence of the grave is shattered! The doom of death defied! The Lion's loud roar echoes backward through yesterday and forward into tomorrow! *"He has risen!"*

Despair turns to delight. A grieving Mary Magdalene clasps her Master's feet in ecstasy. A distraught Peter looks into the loving eyes of the Lord he had denied. Weary Emmaus travelers race joyfully back to Jerusalem in wonder. And a doubtful Thomas touches the scars of his Savior and trusts.

All of history and eternity hinge on the resurrection. The promise from Friday's death was secured by Sunday's life. Because Jesus lives, we too can live—as His, forever. Easter matters today. Easter matters every day.

"Come and see!" The tomb is empty.
"Come and see!" Our Savior lives.

Celebrate! Revel! Rejoice!
Christ is risen! He is risen indeed!

REFERENCES

Verses are listed in the order of their appearance in each reflection.

Reflection 1

Genesis 3:1&4
Genesis 3:21

Reflection 3

Mark 15:31
Luke 22:42

Reflection 4

Luke 4:30

Reflection 5

Matthew 4:19
Matthew 4:20

Reflection 6

John 2:4
John 2:11

Reflection 8

John 3:2
John 3:3
John 3:19
John 3:19&21

Reflection 9

John 4:4

Reflection 10

Luke 7:12-14
Luke 7:16

Reflection 11

Matthew 14:26
Matthew 14:27
(The Message)
Matthew 14:28

Matthew 14:29
  (The Message)
Matthew 14:30

Reflection 12

Mark 8:27
Matthew 16:14
Matthew 16:15
Matthew 16:15

Reflection 13

Luke 9:28
Luke 9:32

Reflection 14

John 8:4-5
John 8:6
John 8:7
John 8:10-11
John 8:11

Reflection 15

John 9:7
John 9:25

Reflection 16

Luke 17:12
Luke 17:13
Luke 17:14
Luke 17:15
Luke 17:17
Luke 17:19

Reflection 17

Luke 19:4

Reflection 18

Matthew 14:21
Matthew 16:16
John 3:4
John 8:7
Matthew 21:10

Reflection 19

Luke 19:44

Reflection 21

Luke 22:8-12

Reflection 22

John 13:4
John 13:8
John 13:7
John 13:5
John 13:12
John 13:13-14

Reflection 23

Luke 22:15-16,19
Matthew 26:27
1 Corinthians 11:24 (KJV)
Luke 22:20
John 19:17-18,34

Reflection 24

John 14:1
John 14:1-3
John 14:2
John 14:18

Reflection 25

John 15:5
John 15:1

Reflection 27

Matthew 26:38
Matthew 26:38
Mark 14:36
Luke 22:42

Reflection 28

Matthew 26:15
Matthew 26:16
John 13:27

Reflection 29

Exodus 3:11
Exodus 3:13
Exodus 3:14
John 18:4
John 18:5
John 18:6

Reflection 30

Matthew 26:63
Matthew 26:64

Reflection 31

Mark 14:29-31 (NLT)
John 13:38
John 18:17
John 18:17
Mark 14:69
Luke 22:58
John 18:26
Mark 14:70
Mark 14:71
Luke 22:61-62

Reflection 32

John 18:37
Matthew 27:19
Matthew 27:23
John 19:5
John 19:14
John 19:15
Matthew 27:24

Reflection 34

John 19:19
John 19:22
John 19:19

Matthew 1:21
John 3:16
Psalm 111:10

Reflection 35

Luke 23:39
Luke 23:40-41
Luke 23:42
Luke 23:43

Reflection 36

Romans 6:23
2 Corinthians 5:21
John 19:30
John 19:30

Reflection 37

Leviticus 16:2
Matthew 27:50-51

Reflection 40

Luke 24:6
Luke 24:5-6
Matthew 28:6

To order additional copies of

LOVE BEYOND DEGREE

Call Toll-Free (800) 247-6553

or e-mail
orders@selahbooks.com

or order online at
www.selahbooks.com